Title: Cheetahs
R.L.: 5.2
PTS: 0.5
TST: 139966

# Amazing Animals
# Cheetahs

Please visit our Web site, www.garethstevens.com. For a free color catalog of all our high-quality books, call toll free 1-800-542-2595 or fax 1-877-542-2596.

**Library of Congress Cataloging-in-Publication Data**

Albee, Sarah.
 Cheetahs / Sarah Albee and Kate Delaney.
     p. cm. — (Amazing animals)
 Includes index.
 ISBN 978-1-4339-4011-8 (pbk.)
 ISBN 978-1-4339-4012-5 (6-pack)
 ISBN 978-1-4339-4010-1 (library binding)
 1.  Cheetah—Juvenile literature.  I. Delaney, Kate. II. Title.
 QL737.C23A398 2010
 599.75'9—dc22
                                    2010000491

This edition first published in 2011 by
**Gareth Stevens Publishing**
111 East 14th Street, Suite 349
New York, NY 10003

This edition copyright © 2011 Gareth Stevens Publishing.
Original edition copyright © 2006 by Readers' Digest Young Families.

Editor: Greg Roza
Designer: Christopher Logan

Photo credits: Cover, back cover, pp. 17 (jaguar and leopard), 44–45, 46 Shutterstock.com; pp. 1, 3, 10–11 © ImageState; pp. 4–5, 24–25, 35 (bottom) © Dynamic Graphics, Inc.; pp. 6–7 © Dreamstime.com/dndavis; pp. 8–9, 12–13, 16–17, 26–27, 32 (bottom left) Photodisc/Getty Images; pp. 14–15, 18 (bottom left), 20–21, 22–23, 25 (bottom right), 26 (bottom left), 28–29, 36–37, 40–41 © JupiterImages; pp. 18–19 © Corbis Corporation; pp. 30–31, 32–33, 34–35, 38–39 © Nova Development Corporation.

Printed in the United States of America

CPSIA compliance information: Batch #CS10GS: For further information contact Gareth Stevens, New York, New York at 1-800-542-2595.

# Amazing Animals
# Cheetahs

By Sarah Albee and Kate Delaney

**Gareth Stevens**
Publishing

# Contents

# Chapter 1
# A Cheetah Story

## Waiting for Spots

Cheetahs are not born with their spots. The dark spots appear gradually and are usually all visible by the time cheetahs are 4 months old.

It was a hot day on a wide-open plain in east Africa. Little Cheetah stretched and yawned. She was lying in the shade alongside her mother and brothers, resting during the heat of the day. The cubs were now almost 4 months old. Mama Cheetah had been keeping a watchful eye out while they slept.

One of Little Cheetah's brothers flicked his tail as he slept. Little Cheetah watched it for a while before pouncing. Her brother woke up and bopped her with his paw. Soon all the cubs were awake, rolling around and playing. They loved to play!

Mama Cheetah stood up and stretched her long, slim legs. She looked around carefully, always alert for lions, hawks, or other **predators** that might want to harm her little ones.

Mama Cheetah walked quietly away in search of food for her family. Suddenly, she made a deep sound that meant, "Stay down, stay put, and be quiet!" The cubs had learned that danger was never very far away.

Mama Cheetah usually stayed within sight of the cubs when she hunted. Today, however, she was gone for hours. Little Cheetah's tummy felt empty. The cubs had big appetites, and Mama Cheetah had to hunt every day to get them food. The cubs no longer drank her milk, so they needed meat to survive. Mama could go 4 or 5 days without food, but the cubs could not.

At last, Mama Cheetah returned, but she had found no food. Everyone went to sleep hungry. When the cubs opened their eyes the next morning, they did not feel like playing. They were very hungry. Mama Cheetah hurried off. She knew she had to find food soon or the cubs would die.

Little Cheetah fell asleep. When she awoke, the sun was high in the sky. Mama Cheetah had returned with food! She let the hungry cubs eat first while she rested from her hunt.

### Wild Words

The word *cheetah* comes from the Hindu word *chia*, which means "spotted one."

### Playing Rough

Rough play is part of growing up in a cheetah family. As cheetah cubs grow older, they chase each other as if they were **prey**. They even practice knocking each other down.

## Home of Her Own

When it's time for a female cheetah to be on her own, she locates her new territory in a place that is very far away from her mother's territory.

Mama Cheetah spent most of her time teaching the cubs how to hunt. She taught them how to move smoothly and noiselessly through the tall grass. She taught them how to stand as still as statues, even on the open plain.

The cubs watched Mama Cheetah chase animals and pounce on them. Sometimes they ran with her and helped her hold the prey down until it died. Mama Cheetah often brought a live hare or antelope calf back to the cubs so they could practice hunting.

When Little Cheetah was about a year old, she and her brothers knew enough about hunting to try it on their own. Sometimes they caught an animal and sometimes they didn't. If they didn't, Mama always shared her food with them.

As time passed, Little Cheetah didn't need help hunting. Mama Cheetah had taught her well. Now it was time for Little Cheetah to find her own territory and be on her own. Little Cheetah bounded away on her long, strong legs. Soon she would start a family of her own.

# Chapter 2

# The Body of a Cheetah

Some scientists think the black lines under the cheetah's eyes reduce the glare of the sun for daytime hunting.

# Spot the Differences

At a quick glance, cheetahs, jaguars, and leopards look alike. All three of these "big cats" have dark spots on gold-colored fur. The cheetah has a black line that runs from the inside corner of each eye to the corner of its mouth below. These lines are called "tear lines."

The spots on cheetahs look like polka dots. The spots on both jaguars and leopards are less regular, forming rosette patterns here and there. The jaguar always has small spots within its rosettes, while the leopard doesn't.

The cheetah has a lean, sleek body and long, slim legs. The leopard and jaguar are thicker and sturdier. The cheetah also has an especially long tail, with black rings near the end.

**The jaguar lives in North and South America.**

**The leopard lives in Africa and Asia.**

# Common Senses

The cheetah's sleek body is designed to run very fast for short distances. Long, slender bones and a **flexible** spine allow the cheetah to take long, rapid strides. Using its powerful hind legs, a cheetah can "get going" faster than a sports car! A cheetah can cover about 27 feet (8.2 m) in a single racing stride.

Cheetahs have been known to run up to 70 miles (113 km) per hour for a distance of about 100 yards (91 m). Even a fast racehorse can only run up to 43 miles (69 km) per hour!

The cheetah's large lungs, heart, and nostrils allow it to use lots of oxygen, helping it move at high speeds. In addition, the cheetah's small ears cut down on **wind resistance**, and its long tail helps it stay balanced.

**Zoom!**

Cheetahs are the fastest land mammals on Earth.

During a chase, the cheetah's legs are completely off the ground when they stretch out. They are completely off the ground again when they meet under its body to start the next stride.

A cheetah's eyesight is so sharp it can spot another animal almost 3 miles (5 km) away.

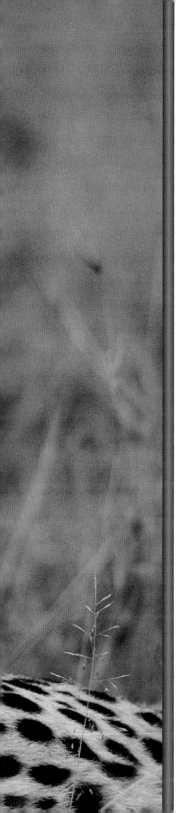

# The Eyes Spy

Cheetahs have excellent vision. Because their eyes face forward, cheetahs are very good at judging the distance to their prey. Most of the prey that cheetahs hunt—such as gazelles, antelope, and hares—have eyes on the sides of their heads. Animals with side-facing eyes are able to spot predators creeping up from behind, so cheetahs must choose the moment to attack very carefully.

Like all cats, cheetahs have excellent senses of smell and hearing. But they do not depend on them for hunting.

# Good Grips

The cheetah's narrow paws have hard, ridged pads on the bottom, like the soles on sneakers. These pads help the cheetah grip the ground when running.

Although a cheetah can pull in its claws, the claws are always exposed. The claws act like spikes on a sprinter's shoes, helping the cheetah get a fast start. The claws continue to grip the ground as the cheetah runs and even help it increase its speed.

# Chapter 3
# The Hunter and the Hunted

## Prey Picks

Cheetahs hunt a variety of animals, such as impalas, young wildebeests, zebras, hares, and the young of almost any animal. The Thomson gazelle, a small antelope, is their favorite.

**The cheetah singles out one animal in a herd as its prey. And it will chase that animal even if another member of the herd is closer.**

# The Plan of Attack

Like all cats, cheetahs are carnivores (KAHR-nuh-vohrz), which means they are meat eaters. But unlike most of the other big cats, which usually hunt at night, the cheetah hunts alone during the day. Only about half of a cheetah's hunting attempts are successful.

The cheetah spends most of the day looking for prey. It will stand motionless for hours in the tall grasses, waiting for prey. Then it will choose one and creep up quietly. When the prey is about 100 feet (30 m) away, the cheetah will spring forward. The cheetah will knock the animal off balance by whacking its rear. Then the cheetah swiftly clamps its jaw onto the animal's neck, crushing its throat. If the animal escapes, it will take the cheetah another hour or two to recover enough strength for another try.

## Hold On!

The cheetah has to keep its tight grip on the neck of its prey until the prey dies. That can take up to 10 minutes. It is during this time other animals try to steal the cheetah's prey.

# Avoiding Danger

Cheetahs are timid animals that try to avoid fights. Their spotted coats act as **camouflage**, hiding them from predators as well as prey. Crouching in tall grass, a cheetah blends in perfectly with its surroundings. It is able to peer out from its hiding place without risk of being seen by other animals.

After a successful hunt, a cheetah eats as soon as it has recovered from the effects of the high-speed chase, but that takes at least 30 minutes. During that time, and even while eating, the cheetah must be on the watch for animals that would steal its prey, especially lions and hyenas. Some animals even follow a stalking cheetah, knowing they can steal its kill without a fight.

Cheetahs have only a few ways to defend themselves. Sometimes they pretend to be fierce by hissing and snarling. But a cheetah's best defense is its ability to run away!

The cheetah will often freeze in its tracks to avoid a fight.

## Chapter 4
# Cheetah Living

Cheetahs are the only big cats that cannot roar.

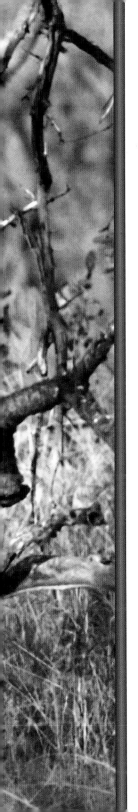

# Lone Rangers

Unlike the members of most other cat families, cheetahs are not very social animals. Female cheetahs almost always live alone except when raising cubs. A male cheetah, on the other hand, will sometimes form a lifelong bond with two or three other males, usually his brothers. These small groups are called **coalitions** (koh-uh-LIH-shunz). Fewer than half of all male cheetahs are members of coalitions.

Coalitions and solitary cheetahs establish their territory by marking the area with **urine**. But cheetahs don't seem to defend territories. Their territories overlap, and the boundaries tend to change along with the travels of their favorite prey. A female's territory is usually much larger than a male's.

# Cheetah Chat

Cheetah's don't roar. They growl or hiss to scare away other animals. Mother cheetahs make loud yelps to call their young and then follow up with low-pitched sounds. Members of a coalition contact each other with yipping sounds. All cheetahs purr when they rest and when they clean themselves. Young cheetahs purr while playing.

# Single Moms

When a female cheetah is ready to mate, her urine has a special scent that attracts males. Male cheetahs are usually very peaceful, but they may fight over the right to mate with a female. After mating, the male and female do not form a family.

The female gives birth about 3 months later. Cheetah cubs are small and blind at birth. They weigh less than 1 pound (0.45 kg), and their eyes don't open until they are about 10 days old. The mother leaves her babies every day to hunt for food. Cubs are in great danger when they are alone. The mother moves them to a different hiding place every couple of days. Even so, only one of every 20 cheetah cubs born in the wild will live to become an adult.

### Fuzzy Wuzzy

Fuzzy grayish hairs grow along the heads and backs of cheetah cubs. The growth is called a mantle. It helps hide the cubs in the grass. Cubs lose their mantles as they grow older, but some males carry traces of their mantles all their lives.

A mother cheetah may give birth to as many as six to eight cubs at a time, but the average litter has three or four cubs.

When young cheetahs play-hunt, they pounce, stalk, and run as fast as they can. This kind of playing helps strengthen the muscles they will need for real hunting.

# Hunters in Training

A mother cheetah has many important jobs. One is to keep her cubs alive. Another is to teach them how to hunt so they can keep themselves alive. By the time cubs are 6 weeks old, they follow their mother on hunts. She has them stay out of sight from predators but in a place where she can keep an eye on them.

As babies, the cubs drink only their mother's milk. But when they are around 3 months old, they start to eat meat, which their mother chews up for them. By the time they are 6 months old, the cubs eat only meat.

The cubs stay very still and watch their mother stand on mounds of earth and fallen trees to search for prey. They watch how she moves when she stalks prey and how she races after it and bites it. Sometimes she brings back live prey so they can practice hunting.

When they are about 1 year old, the cubs go off on their own hunts or hunt as a group. One day, when they are about 16 months old, they don't return. They may stay together as a group for a few more months, and then the females will go off on their own.

# Chapter 5
## Cheetahs in the World

# Cheetahs in History

People have been taming cheetahs since ancient times. A Greek vase from around 2500 B.C. has a picture of a cheetah wearing a collar. Later on, tamed cheetahs were used for hunting in parts of the Middle East, India, Asia, and Africa. There are even reports that King George III of England hunted with cheetahs in the late eighteenth century.

After people captured a cheetah, they tamed it by giving it small amounts of food over a period of time. Eventually the cheetah came to trust the person who fed it. Owners walked tamed cheetahs with a collar and leash just like we do with dogs today. Because they almost never mate in **captivity** and are in danger of **extinction**, cheetahs are no longer tamed.

## Fast Facts About Cheetahs

| | |
|---|---|
| **Scientific name** | *Acinonyx jubatus* |
| **Order** | Carnivora |
| **Family** | Felidae |
| **Size** | 30 inches (76 cm) tall at the shoulder |
| | 44 to 53 inches (112 to 135 cm) long |
| **Length of tail** | 26 to 33 inches (66 to 84 cm) |
| **Weight** | 80 to 150 pounds (36 to 68 kg) |
| **Life Span** | About 8 years |
| **Habitat** | Grasslands |

# What Happened?

Cheetahs have most of the problems other **endangered** animals do. But cheetahs also have a problem that most other animals do not. A major source of concern to scientists is inbreeding, which means the mating of cheetahs that are too closely related.

Scientists believe something occurred about 10,000 years ago that killed a large number of cheetahs. It might have been a dramatic climate change. After this huge reduction in their population, cheetahs had fewer mates to choose from, and they had to mate with relatives. As a result, all cheetahs today are very much alike **genetically**.

Because cheetahs share so many genetic similarities, they are at great risk of being wiped out completely by disease. If a serious disease broke out within another species, it would not necessarily be a danger to every member of the group because they are not so similar genetically. However, a disease that affects one cheetah is likely to affect most cheetahs.

## A Different Kind

King cheetahs have big, dark blotches instead of spots, and dark stripes run down their spines. King cheetahs are not a separate species. They are the result of an unusual **gene** that is carried by both parents.

King cheetahs are very rare. There are probably no more than 30 in the world.

# Where Cheetahs Live

EUROPE

ASIA

AFRICA

Iran

Algeria

Niger

Chad

Eritrea

Sudan

Djibouti

Senegal

Mali

Guinea

Ethiopia

Nigeria

Somalia

Burkina Faso

Ghana

Benin

Uganda

Togo

Kenya

Cameroon

Dem. Rep. of Congo

Central African Republic

Tanzania

Angola

Mozambique

Zambia

Namibia

Malawi

South Africa

Zimbabwe

Botswana

The **light green** areas show where cheetahs live.

# Cheetahs in Danger

Cheetahs are the most endangered of all the big cat species. They once lived throughout Africa and Asia. However, today most cheetahs live in eastern and southwestern Africa. The largest numbers live in Namibia. There are probably only 12,000 to 14,000 cheetahs in the wild today.

As is the case with so many other animals, the destruction of habitat and the actions of humans are the major reasons why cheetahs are endangered. When their habitat is taken away or changed, so are the prey that live there. When there are no prey, then there is no way for the cheetah to survive. When ranchers move into an area, the cheetah is unable to tell the difference between wild prey and farm animals. In order to defend their herds, ranchers believe they have the right to kill cheetahs.

Although trading in cheetah fur has long been illegal, **poachers** know they can find buyers for the beautiful furs. The more endangered the cheetah becomes, the more money poachers can get for the furs. The threats against cheetahs don't paint a rosy picture for their future. We must do all we can to protect the cheetah and its natural habitat.

# Glossary

camouflage—colors or shapes in animals that allow them to hide in their habitat

captivity—the state of being caged

coalition—a small group of male cheetahs, often brothers, that stay together for life

endangered—a species of animal or plant in danger of dying out

extinction—the death of all members of a species

flexible—able to be bent without breaking

gene—a tiny unit of a cell that is passed along from parent to child and that determines specific traits such as eye color

genetically—relating to genes

habitat—the natural environment where an animal or plant lives

poacher—a person who illegally kills or captures wild animals

predator—an animal that hunts and eats other animals to survive

prey—animals that are hunted by other animals for food

urine—a yellow liquid containing water and waste products that flows out of an animal's body

wind resistance—a force that works against a moving object. It is caused by air hitting the object as it moves

# Cheetahs: Show What You Know

How much have you learned about cheetahs? Grab a piece of paper and a pencil and write down your answers.

1. What facial feature sets cheetahs apart from jaguars and leopards?

2. How fast can a cheetah run?

3. On which sense does the cheetah depend most when hunting?

4. After catching prey, how does a cheetah kill it

5. When is an adult cheetah most defenseless?

6. What is a cheetah's best defense?

7. What is the fuzzy grayish hair on the heads and backs of cheetah cubs called?

8. How many cheetah cubs are in an average litter?

9. About how old are cheetahs when they leave their mothers to live on their own?

10. What are the three greatest dangers to cheetahs today?

1. Black lines that run from the inside corners of the eyes to the corners of the mouth, called "tear lines" 2. About 70 miles (113 km) an hour 3. Sight 4. Crushing the prey's windpipe with its jaws 5. Just after a successful hunt when it must protect its catch 6. Running away 7. The mantle 8. Three or four 9. 16 months 10. Inbreeding, destruction of natural habitat, and poachers

# For More Information

## Books

Hanel, Rachael. *Cheetahs*. Mankato, MN: Creative Education, 2010.

Harkrader, Lisa. *The Cheetah*. Berkeley Heights, NJ: MyReportLinks.com Books, 2005.

MacMillan, Dianne M. *Cheetahs*. Minneapolis, MN: Lerner Publishing, 2009.

## Web Sites

### National Geographic Kids: Creature Feature—Cheetahs
*kids.nationalgeographic.com/Animals/CreatureFeature/Cheetah*
Browse numerous cheetah resources, including facts, photos, maps, and video.

### Cheetah Kids
*www.cheetahkids.com*
Learn about cheetahs and what people can do to save them from extinction.

**Publisher's note to educators and parents**: Our editors have carefully reviewed these Web sites to ensure that they are suitable for students. Many Web sites change frequently, however, and we cannot guarantee that a site's future contents will continue to meet our high standards of quality and educational value. Be advised that students should be closely supervised whenever they access the Internet.

# Index